FOREWORD

Asexual Outreach is committed to supporting ace (asexual spectrum) youth, and this ace inclusion guide is a manifestation of that support. This guide features resources for LGBTQ+ clubs, educators, guidance counselors, and administrators who wish to support ace youth in their schools and communities. This resource kit will give you the tools you need to make spaces inclusive for ace students at your school.

This Ace Inclusion Guide for High Schools is just one of Asexual Outreach's many programs designed to promote ace inclusivity, equity, education, and awareness in our communities. To help you further promote ace awareness at your school, our ace inclusion and awareness workshop series can be brought to your school or to your school board. Whether you're looking for an ace equity and inclusion workshop for your LGBTQ+ club, looking for an ace presenter for a school assembly or ace event, or looking for a workshop to train your school's staff in ace inclusion, equity, and awareness, we can send someone to help you achieve those goals. For further information on how to bring a presenter from Asexual Outreach to your school or community group, and for further information on how you can get involved, contact us by email at **schools@asexualoutreach.org** or by phone (toll-free) at **1-855-5-ASEXUAL (1-855-527-3982)**.

Throughout this book, look for links to further resources on **http://schools.asexualoutreach.org/** where you can find more nuanced information.

WHO WE ARE

Asexual Outreach is a 501(c)(3) non-profit organization building a national advocacy movement to strengthen communities and change lives. By providing structure, sustainability, and resources that help communities and projects flourish, we help empower communities and advocates to make a difference.

Since 2014, we have worked to support ace youth through partnerships with LGBTQ+ youth-serving organizations, through school workshops and trainings, and through resources like this book. As a growing number of aces are coming out in their middle-school and high-school years, support for those youth is becoming increasingly needed. To help address this need, Asexual Outreach works with local community groups across Canada and the United States to help them create change on a local level, and works with school boards and with LGBTQ+ organizations to help them build ace inclusion into their programs and services.

We created this book to help people take ace inclusion into their own hands, and we hope that you find it useful in building that inclusion yourself.

ACKNOWLEDGMENTS

This Ace Inclusion Guide for High Schools could not have been created without the generosity of our supporters and colleagues, nor could it exist without the knowledge and resources built up by the ace community since the early 2000's.

The initial development of these books was funded by the generosity of our supporters, and to them, we are incredibly grateful. We are immensely appreciative for all of the volunteers who helped with the development of these books and for all of those whom we consulted with along the way. We especially acknowledge the direct contributions of CJ Chasin, Eriol S., and other members of Ace Toronto who were instrumental in the development of this book from its onset.

About This Book

ABOUT THIS BOOK

This book features a comprehensive introduction to the asexual spectrum in the first chapter, as well as a much lengthier glossary at the end of the book where you can discover definitions to terms that you may encounter. Given these two together, you should be well on your way to understanding, including, and supporting aces at your school.

To help further, the second chapter of this book will help students make their school's LGBTQ+ club into an inclusive and welcoming space for aces, and the third chapter of this book will help them extend that inclusion across their school.

This book additionally contains chapters for educators, for guidance counselors, and for administrators at your school. With chapters targeted specifically for each position, your school staff will learn how they can best support aces in their staff roles.

⚡ As the ace community and movement continually evolve, concepts and terms that exist in this book may eventually fall out of fashion, while others will certainly emerge. This book is not meant to be a definitive, eternal guide to navigating ace students, but rather to be a starting point for ace inclusion.

As the ace community and the language it uses evolve, Asexual Outreach will evolve with it, and will help you to follow along by continually updating this book's accompanying online resource: http://schools.asexualoutreach.org/

About This Book

If you're involved in your school's LGBTQ+ club, or are a student looking to make your school a more ace-friendly space, take a look at chapter 1, *"An Introduction to the Asexual Spectrum"*, chapter 2, *"Including Aces in Your LGBTQ+ Club"*, and chapter 3, *"Creating an Ace-Friendly School"* and keep the glossary at the end of this book handy should you ever encounter new terms or want to learn more.

If you are an educator, take a look at both chapter 1, *"An Introduction to the Asexual Spectrum"*, and chapter 4, *"Resources and Information for Educators"*.

If you are a guidance counselor, check out both chapter 1, *"An Introduction to the Asexual Spectrum"*, and chapter 5, *"Resources and Information for Guidance Counselors"*.

If you are an administrator, take a look at both chapter 1, *"An Introduction to the Asexual Spectrum"*, and chapter 6, *"Resources and Information for Administrators"*.

If you're not an educator, guidance counselor, or administrator, give these sections to the staff at your school! To more easily distribute these sections, PDF and print versions can be found online at **http://schools.asexualoutreach.org/guide/**

Throughout this book as well, look for links to further resources on **http://schools.asexualoutreach.org/** where you can find up to date and more nuanced information.

Chapters in this Book

CHAPTERS IN THIS BOOK

1. AN INTRODUCTION TO THE ASEXUAL SPECTRUM

This chapter is a comprehensive guide to the asexual spectrum, and will help you to understand the ace community so that you can familiarize yourself with this diverse group in order to better support them.

2. INCLUDING ACES IN YOUR LGBTQ+ CLUB

This chapter will give you many of the tools you need to include aces in your school's LGBTQ+ club. It will help you to ensure ace inclusion, to support aces who join your group, and to run ace education and inclusion activities for your club.

3. CREATING AN ACE-FRIENDLY SCHOOL

This chapter will help you take the first steps toward making your school a safer space for aces.

✂ Feel free to detach any of the chapters found within this book, photocopy them, and/or distribute copies to staff and students in your school. You can additionally find printable versions of each section at http://schools.asexualoutreach.org/guide/

Chapters in this Book

4. ACE INFORMATION AND RESOURCES FOR EDUCATORS

This chapter will help educators to understand aces, to support them, and to include them in their classrooms and their teaching.

5. ACE INFORMATION AND RESOURCES FOR GUIDANCE COUNSELORS

This chapter will help guidance counselors at your school understand and support ace students.

6. ACE INFORMATION AND RESOURCES FOR ADMINISTRATORS

This chapter will help administrators in your school understand the need for school wide support for ace students, and understand how to support aces who are struggling with bullying and finding acceptance.

7. ACE INCLUSIVE SEXUAL EDUCATION

This chapter will help sex educators understand the need for ace inclusive sexual education, and will help them implement ace inclusivity in their teaching and curricula.

8. GLOSSARY

This section contains a comprehensive glossary of terms and concepts related to the asexual spectrum, and will act as a reference guide for any new terms that you may come across.

This Ace Inclusion Guide for High Schools is a part of *Asexual Outreach's* larger youth outreach programming. Further school resources, including a digital copy of this entire guide, can be found at ***http://schools.asexualoutreach.org/***
For additional help including aces in your school and classes or to bring a speaker to your school, you can contact us by email at ***schools@asexualoutreach.org*** or by phone *(toll-free)* at ***1-855-5-ASEXUAL (1-855-527-3982)***.

AN INTRODUCTION TO THE ASEXUAL SPECTRUM

CHAPTER 1

ⓘ This Ace Inclusion Guide for High Schools is a part of *Asexual Outreach's* larger youth outreach programming. Further school resources, including a digital copy of this entire guide, can be found at ***http://schools.asexualoutreach.org/***
For additional help including aces in your school and classes or to bring a speaker to your school, you can contact us by email at ***schools@asexualoutreach.org*** or by phone *(toll-free)* at ***1-855-5-ASEXUAL (1-855-527-3982)***.

INTRODUCTION

This chapter will provide you with a comprehensive understanding of the asexual spectrum, so that you can familiarize yourself with the diverse ace community in order to better support them.

This chapter will cover:

- **The Asexual Spectrum**
- **Types of Attraction**
- **Sex Drive and Arousal**
- **Issues Aces Face**
- **Issues That Aces in Your School May Face**
- **Where Aces Fit in the LGBTQ+ Community**

The Asexual Spectrum

THE ASEXUAL SPECTRUM

Asexuality is a sexual orientation, and it generally describes a lack of sexual attraction and/or a lack of sexual desire. Sexuality is a spectrum and the umbrella term for individuals who identify toward the asexual end of the spectrum is ace. As such, "ace" encompasses many people including those who experience no sexual attraction, those who experience no sexual desire, and those who do experience sexual attraction, but infrequently enough that they still identify with the ace community.

Numerous identities fall on the asexual spectrum; while there are too many to adequately list here, the following page contains examples of ace identities:

> **!** There is no one way that people come to an ace identity, and while some people may feel like they were always asexual, some people come to their ace identity through other experiences. Many aces have disabilities, are neurodivergent, have hormonal conditions, and/or have survived sexual assault. Some aces come to identify with the asexual spectrum via these experiences, and this does not make their identity any less valid than any other sexual identity. All aces' identities must be respected.

As people have begun more closely discerning different types of attraction, new labels have emerged to describe the diverse experiences that many in the ace community have. Because new labels continue to emerge, you can visit http://schools.asexualoutreach.org/gray-area/ for an up to date list and discussion.

The Asexual Spectrum

IDENTITIES ON THE ASEXUAL SPECTRUM

The following three identities are some of the most common within the ace community, and were the first identities to emerge in the ace community.

→ **Asexual:** a person who experiences little or no sexual attraction to anyone, and/or does not experience desire for sexual contact.

→ **Demisexual:** a person who can only experience sexual attraction if a strong emotional bond is present. Although this bond is a prerequisite for attraction, it is not a guarantee that attraction will occur.

→ **Gray-asexual (or graysexual):** a person who experiences sexual attraction rarely, only under specific circumstances, without libido/sex-drive, or without enough strength to act on that attraction. This can also describe someone who fluctuates between periods of experiencing sexual attraction and periods of not experiencing sexual attraction.

Q: *What word could I use to describe people who don't identify on the asexual spectrum?*

A: **Z-sexual** describes those who do not identify on the asexual spectrum. The term was coined in order to convey the idea of a spectrum (from A to Z) and not to set ace in opposition to non-ace, which would imply that "non-ace" was the default. Another common term for someone who doesn't identify on the sexual spectrum is **allosexual**.

Types of Attraction

TYPES OF ATTRACTION

Attraction is the basis for determining orientation for a lot of people—both what gender(s) they experience attraction toward and the circumstances under which said attraction is experienced. Although aces tend to experience little or no sexual attraction, many still experience different types of attraction toward other people. In order to better describe these experiences, the early ace community distinguished different 'types' of attraction, creating a model for separating orientations based on these types of attraction. (This is known as the "split-orientation model").

The first type of attraction to be coined was "romantic attraction" - because many aces desire some form of romantic relationship, this type of attraction is commonly discussed within ace communities. Other types of attraction have been coined, and some of the most common are outlined over the next few pages. It is important to note, however, that these types of attraction and their corresponding orientations are based on an imperfect model and do not fit within everyone's experience.

SEXUAL ATTRACTION

Sexual attraction describes how one is drawn to others "sexually", and often results in a desire for sexual contact with those others. It is commonly defined as a sexual urge that is directed at or caused by a specific person, a specific gender, or specific genders that occurs outside of a sexual situation or context. However, sexual desire is distinct from sexual attraction; in fact, some aces experience sexual desire outside of sexual attraction.

This type of attraction is what most people base their orientations off of. For example, many people who identify as gay would be considered homosexual, and thus experience sexual attraction exclusively to the same sex or gender. The same follows for many other orientations, including straight, bi, pan, and even ace. However, because many aces experience attraction aside from sexual attraction, many find it useful to also/instead identify with a romantic orientation.

Sexual attraction is often felt alongside other types of attraction such as romantic attraction (which will be explored on the next page).

Types of Attraction

ROMANTIC ATTRACTION

Romantic attraction describes how one is drawn to others in a strictly "romantic" way. As with sexual attraction, people who experience romantic attraction often experience it toward a specific gender or toward multiple genders. This pattern of romantic attraction is called romantic orientation.

Each sexual orientation that exists has a corresponding romantic orientation, and for many people these two align (for example, many bisexual people are also biromantic). However, this is not always the case, especially among aces. The terminology for discussing romantic orientation came from the ace community's need to differentiate between these two types of attraction.

 A crush is a strong desire for a romantic relationship caused by being romantically attracted to someone. This is distinct from a squish - a platonic crush that we will explore more in the platonic attraction section!

As sexual and romantic orientations do not always align, not all aromantic people also identify as ace, and with romantic attraction becoming more widely known, aromantic people are beginning to form their own communities and discourse outside of the ace community.

As with gray-asexuality, there is now a vast diversity of labels to describe the experiences that people on the aromantic spectrum have. Because new labels continue to emerge, you can visit http://schools.asexualoutreach.org/gray-area/ for an up to date list and discussion.

Types of Attraction

Some aces experience romantic attraction, even though they might not experience sexual attraction. Many others do not experience romantic attraction, and many find they do not identify as either a romantic or as romantic - like sexuality, romanticism is a spectrum. The following are few examples of aromantic spectrum identities:

→ **Aromantic:** a person who does not experience romantic attraction to anyone.

→ **Demiromantic:** a person who can only experience romantic attraction if a strong emotional bond is present.

→ **Gray-aromantic (or grayromantic):** often used to describe someone who falls between aromantic and romantic. Some people also use quoiromantic and other labels to express that they experience romantic attraction but that it is nebulous and difficult to identify how that attraction works.

The following is a chart of romantic orientations found within the ace community, based on a 2014 census.

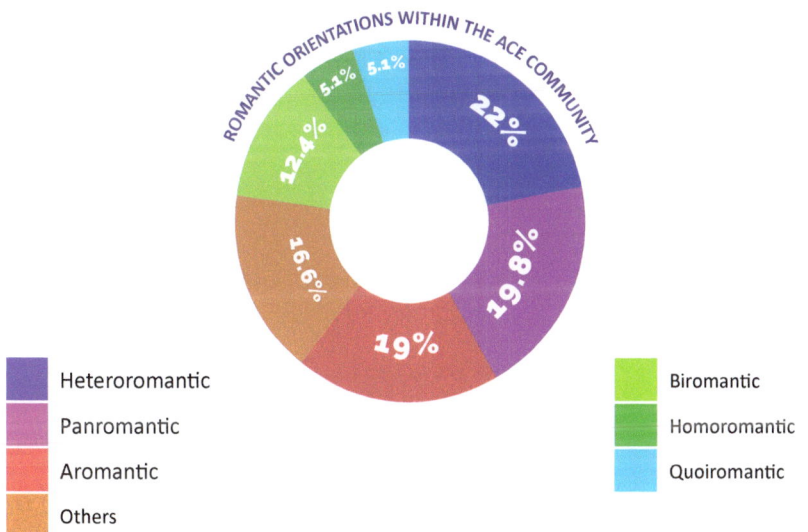

SOURCE: GINOZA, M. K., & MILLER, T. (2014, NOVEMBER 1). *THE 2014 AVEN COMMUNITY CENSUS: PRELIMINARY FINDINGS.*

Ace Inclusion Guide for High Schools

Types of Attraction

PLATONIC ATTRACTION

Platonic attraction relates to the desire to deeply know someone or to befriend someone in a way that is more emotionally intimate than a typical friendship. This attraction is non-sexual and non-romantic in nature, but results in the desire to be around someone in a friendly capacity. Despite not experiencing romantic attraction, many aromantic people do experience platonic attraction.

> A squish is the platonic variation of a crush and thus is a strong desire to form a close platonic relationship with someone. The envisioned relationship often takes the form of a deep friendship or a queerplatonic relationship - a non-romantic relationship beyond what most would consider a friendship.

AESTHETIC ATTRACTION

Aesthetic attraction is an appreciation of or an attraction toward a person's surface level attributes that is not necessarily connected to sexual, romantic, or platonic desires. This attraction is commonly compared to the appreciation of artwork - while it is enjoyable to look at, one does not necessarily experience sexual attraction toward it.

SEX DRIVE AND AROUSAL

Libido, or sex drive, refers to a psychological desire for sexual activity and/or sexual pleasure. This desire can emerge alongside or independent of sexual attraction; therefore, many aces can experience libido. As with non-ace people, aces' sex drives vary widely: some aces have no libido, some have a very high libido, and others lie in between the two.

Where sex drive is a psychological phenomenon, arousal is a physical response to stimuli. Like sex drive, it does not necessarily lead to sexual activity, and can vary in intensity and frequency. Some aces experience sex drive and arousal, and some aces choose to engage in sexual activity, often as a result of these two experiences. Some aces may choose to have sex with others, and this sexual activity does not in any way negate their orientation or identity.

Because of compulsory sexuality - the pervasive belief that everyone past a certain age experiences sexual attraction and that everyone can and should engage in sexual activity – and because intimate relationships are often assumed to be sexual, aces can face a lot of pressure from partners, peers, and others to engage in sexual activities that they may be uncomfortable with, and this can lead to sexual assault and rape. While some aces do enjoy and engage in sexual activity, it is always essential to note that not all aces are interested in sex, that an ace's decision not to have sex must always be respected, regardless of circumstance, and that aces never owe partners sex and should never be pressured or coerced into unwanted sexual activity.

Sex Drive And Arousal

> **!** This section applies more broadly than just to aces; in fact, nobody should ever be pressured into having sex, and every choice not to have sex must always be respected, regardless of sexual orientation or circumstance. Consider discussing consent at a LGBTQ+ club meeting so that this vital topic can reach the members of your group! If sex education at your school does not currently discuss consent, consider advocating for this topic's inclusion.

Because behavior does not determine or always represent attraction, some aces do masturbate – often for many of the same reasons that non-aces do. Additionally, some aces are interested in and engage in kink/BDSM because these do not necessarily require sexual activity. Some aces practice kink/BDSM without involving sexual activity, while some (and often the same) do involve sexual activity.

In sum, aces are diverse in their experiences, interests, and behaviors – none of which invalidate their orientation. There is no one way to be ace!

> 💡 While people are sometimes curious about the sexual behaviours and interests of individual aces, it is usually not appropriate to ask people about their sexual behaviours and interests. Many people are not comfortable sharing these personal experiences, and they should never be expected to do so.

ISSUES ACES FACE

Because asexuality intersects with other identities in complex ways, the issues that each individual ace person faces are heavily influenced by that individual's other identities.

While aces as a whole face invisibility and invalidation, aces may face further issues depending on their gender identity and gender expression, romantic orientation, dis/ability, race, ethnic origin, socioeconomic status, age, religion, and a variety of other factors. Understanding these intersections is key to understanding the issues that may be impacting aces you know.

The following pages briefly overview many of the issues that aces face. These issues can be incredibly complex and thus cannot be be entirely summarized here. For further information on these and other issues, visit http://schools.asexualoutreach.org/issues/

Issues Aces Face

TRANSPHOBIA AND HOMOPHOBIA

People on the asexual spectrum often have trouble accessing information about their orientation. According to a survey conducted by the Asexual Visibility and Education Network (AVEN) in 2014, 28% of aces are trans and/or non-binary, and most of them experience transphobia and cissexism. The majority of aces also experience homophobia due to their LGBQ+ romantic orientation or aromanticism, or because they are perceived to be LGBTQ+ due to their non-conventional gender presentations.

PATHOLOGIZATION OF THE ASEXUAL SPECTRUM

It's common for medical professionals to "diagnose" aces as mentally or physically ill to explain away their ace identity, and these diagnoses are seemingly justified by major psychological texts that problematically and inaccurately represent the asexual spectrum, ignore it, or deny it altogether.

ERASURE OF INTERSECTING IDENTITIES

Aces who are also members of other marginalized groups often have trouble accessing the ace identity itself, as the group they are part of is systemically hypersexualized or desexualized. For example, aces from Black and Latinx backgrounds are often hypersexualized, while East Asian aces and aces with disabilities are often desexualized and infantilizied. These issues of compulsory sexuality, however, play out for racialized aces in a variety of contradictory ways, and these issues make it especially difficult for racialized aces and aces with disabilities to explore their ace identities, access ace discourse, and have their ace identities acknowledged and respected.

For aces, erasure often comes in the form of the suggestion that ace identities can and should be changed. Sometimes people will only accept an ace's identity after suggesting various possible "causes". The preoccupation with why people are ace or how they came to be that way enforces the belief that an identifiable "cause" delegitimizes ace identities, as well as the belief that it is possible to cure asexuality.

Issues Aces Face

COMPULSORY SEXUALITY

Compulsory sexuality is the pervasive belief that everyone past a certain age can and should want to engage in sexual activity. Compulsory sexuality often defines sexual activity in heterosexual terms; in such instances, it is called "compulsory heterosexuality" and is harmful to aces and other members of the LGBTQ+ community.

The idea that everyone can and should have sex invalidates and erases ace identities, along with those who cannot or do not want to have sex for other reasons (and who may also be ace). It further perpetuates the view that aces should not exist and that there is something wrong with them. When it manifests as compulsory heterosexuality, it furthers homophobic and transphobic ideas about gender, sex, and sexuality.

Members of racialised and colonised communities often have an especially difficult time accessing ace identities due to people who use ideas of compulsory sexuality to deny them their experience. Similarly, women from these communities also suffer when people evoke harmful stereotypes about them based on their ethnic, racial, or cultural background, coupled with sexist expectations of compulsory sexuality.

Compulsory sexuality is sometimes present in LGBTQ+ spaces that are declared to be "sex-positive" when their definition of sex positivity is that sexual activity is inherently empowering and can and should be practiced and enjoyed by everyone. By failing to recognize that sexual activity is not inherently positive and by failing to empower those who do not engage in sexual activity, these spaces can further alienate aces.

HARASSMENT, SEXUAL ASSAULT, AND RAPE

Aces are vulnerable to sexual assault and rape, particularly "corrective" rape where the rapist is trying to "fix" or "cure" their ace identity. Aces are also prone to being victims of rape or sexual coercion where others may manipulate and pressure them to obtain sex. This is particularly common when aces interact with or date non-aces in situations where consent is not properly understood.

> "I figured out I was asexual with a girlfriend in high school. She was really overly sexual, and wanted me to do a lot more stuff than I was really into. She was abusive and emotionally manipulative, and I was afraid of her, so I consented, and I tried to make it seem like I was into it, although I was not."
>
> – Anonymous

INADEQUATE MEDIA REPRESENTATION

While ace awareness is growing, there is still a lack of accurate representation in media. When characters are identified as ace, they're used as comic relief or are "cured" at some point in the storyline. These inaccuracies lead non-aces to make incorrect assumptions.

When aces appear in mainstream media interviews and even when coverage is positive, representation of the ace community remains overwhelmingly white, further alienating aces of color.

ISSUES THAT ACES IN YOUR SCHOOL MAY FACE

Young aces face a unique set of challenges that mostly relate to invalidation and invisibility.

Because few people understand the asexual spectrum, aces in your school will often face difficulties having their orientation legitimized. Often, parents, peers, and teachers and other school staff will not accept a student's ace identity at face value, and instead suggest various incorrect explanations for this student's orientation.

> "I let my mom know, and she told me 'It's a fad for people to label themselves now, you shouldn't label yourself." - Sam

> "As junior year rolled around and I became more and more exposed to relationships and activities like prom, I increasingly felt left out, sick and unneeded – a burden to everyone around me. I went through all the stages of questioning: confusion, withdrawal, self-hate, fear, rejection of others, frustration, and excruciating mental turmoil. My identity crisis took a toll on every aspect of my life. My grades and track performance took a deep hit. And most of all, the question of "Who am I?" plagued me."
> - Emelyn Chiang

Issues That Aces in Your School May Face

INVISIBILITY AND INVALIDATION

For many students, early high school years are a time for exploring sexuality – many constantly question who others "like", who they find attractive, even who they would want to have sex with, and this can be very confusing for aces who may not be experiencing these feelings.

Because of these constant sexual discussions and this normalizing of sexual attraction, many aces are led to feel that they are broken – without knowing the asexual exists, many aces can feel broken and isolated for years, sometimes even for decades. Peers can reinforce this feeling of brokenness by assuming something is wrong with aces.

When aces do discover the ace community and label, accepting this label for themselves can be difficult as many may not want to be associated with what society deems "the other". Coming to identify as ace can also be a difficult process because it can be very difficult for aces to understand what sexual attraction actually is – especially if they do not experience it themselves.

Those who choose to come out as ace often face delegitimization with others assuming their sexuality is a phase, assuming that the ace is a "late bloomer," or believing that the asexual spectrum simply cannot exist. Young aces in particular are often told that they are too young to know that they are ace when, in fact, there is no minimum age to identifying as ace and all aces should be trusted in their identification - even if they are younger.

Given this, many aces might not be accepted or supported by their parents, their families, or their peers, leaving them with few options for support.

Issues That Aces in Your School May Face

BULLYING

Young aces are at a heightened risk of being the victims of bullying compared to their cisgender straight peers, yet schools often lack the tools and resources to deal with ace related bullying. Because many aces have LGBQ+ romantic orientations and/or are aromantic, many are trans and/or non-binary, and many present their gender in non-conventional ways, many young aces are the victims of homophobic and transphobic bullying.

Further still, many young aces are bullied just for being different. They are often called prudes, frigid, and other names/descriptors in an attempt to harm them, and these certainly can be harmful.

They may even be physically and sexually assaulted, and in some extreme cases, can be victims of "corrective" rape.

Ace related bullying might not always be obvious; because not everyone understands the asexual spectrum, many people fail to recognize acephobic bullying. Furthermore, because ace related bullying is not always treated seriously, because aces may not wish to be outed, and because of the shaming inherent in this bullying, this bullying often goes unreported.

Because school administrators often do not understand the asexual spectrum and the issues that aces face, they are often ill-equipped to prevent and stop ace related bullying.

Issues That Aces in Your School May Face

SUPPORT SYSTEMS

Because parents, teachers, and peers often invalidate or dismiss an ace's identity, and because of the extensive lack of ace awareness and acceptance, aces can have difficulties finding support. Because of this, it is essential that your school makes an effort to create supportive and safe spaces for ace students.

> "When I first told my mom, she played the "but I want grandkids" card, which really hurt. Its been six months since I've talked to her about it and now I feel like there is a broken synopsis between us, a conversation we can't have again"
>
> — Anonymous

WHERE ACES FIT IN THE LGBTQ+ COMMUNITY

While there has not been and likely never will be a universal decision, many aces consider themselves to be part of the LGBTQ+ community, and in recent years, many LGBTQ+ organizations and folks have welcomed them into the community.

Identity is complex: many aces identify with an LGBQ+ romantic orientation and many (often the same) aces identify as trans and/or non-binary, and so many aces identify as queer as well.

Regardless of their place in the LGBTQ+ community, many aces do not feel comfortable in a lot of LGBTQ+ spaces, and many of these spaces do not make room for those on the asexual spectrum.

As you may have noticed in the previous pages, aces face a lot of the same issues that others in the LGBTQ+ community face, and for many aces, LGBTQ+ spaces and organizations will be the first that they turn to for help. As such, it is vital that LGBTQ+ spaces do make room for aces and do explicitly support them.

Where Aces Fit in the LGBTQ+ Community

...PSSST!

The *"LGBT"* acronym does not always work for everyone; in fact, some people are critical of it because it does not always adequately include all in the community it purports to represent. (For example, the asexual spectrum is often discluded from this acronym) This inclusion guide uses *"LGBTQ+"* because it is more easily recognizable by those who are not especially familiar with queer discourse; however, there are certainly alternative initialisms and acronyms that are more inclusive.

The following are some examples of these alternatives, each with their own benefits and disadvantages:

- ☐ **GSM:** Gender and Sexual Minorities
- ☐ **GSRM:** Gender, Sexual, and Romantic Minorities
- ☐ **GSD:** Gender and Sexual Diversity
- ☐ **QUILTBAG:** "Queer/Questioning, Undecided, Intersex, Lesbian, Trans, Bisexual, Asexual, Gay/Genderqueer
- ☐ **MOGAI:** Marginalized Orientations, Gender Alignments, and Intersex

> "when large parts of the community insists "a" is for allies not ace/aro it hurts and feels like even in a queer community i am not welcome."
>
> — Ethan

ℹ️ This Ace Inclusion Guide for High Schools is a part of *Asexual Outreach's* larger youth outreach programming. Further school resources, including a digital copy of this entire guide, can be found at ***http://schools.asexualoutreach.org/***
For additional help including aces in your school and classes or to bring a speaker to your school, you can contact us by email at ***schools@asexualoutreach.org*** or by phone *(toll-free)* at ***1-855-5-ASEXUAL (1-855-527-3982)***.

Including Aces In Your LGBTQ+ club

CHAPTER 2

This Ace Inclusion Guide for High Schools is a part of *Asexual Outreach's* larger youth outreach programming. Further school resources, including a digital copy of this entire guide, can be found at ***http://schools.asexualoutreach.org/***
For additional help including aces in your school and classes or to bring a speaker to your school, you can contact us by email at ***schools@asexualoutreach.org*** or by phone *(toll-free)* at ***1-855-5-ASEXUAL (1-855-527-3982)***.

Introduction

Because of the lack of support services for aces and because many aces consider themselves to fall under the LGBTQ+ umbrella, your LGBTQ+ club will likely be the first place that many aces in your school will go. Therefore, making your club ace friendly can be instrumental in changing and bettering the lives of aces in your school and community.

This chapter will cover:

»→ **Making Your LGBTQ+ Club Ace Friendly**

»→ **Ways to Ensure Ace Inclusion**
- *Make Your Inclusion Known*
- *Include Asexuality When Listing Sexual Orientations*
- *Educate LGBTQ+ Club Members on the Asexual Spectrum*
- *Allow People to Change Their Labels*
- *Make No Assumptions*

»→ **Supporting Aces Who Join Your Club**

»→ **Ace Education and Inclusion Activities for Your LGBTQ+ Club**

MAKING YOUR CLUB ACE FRIENDLY

The first step in making your LGBTQ+ club ace friendly is understanding the asexual spectrum yourself. If you are at all unfamiliar with the asexual spectrum, consider reading *"An Introduction to the Asexual Spectrum"* at the start of this book, and encourage your fellow club leaders and any teachers involved in your club to do the same.

The following pages expand on some steps that you can take to ensure that aces are included in your LGBTQ+ club.

These steps include:

- Making your inclusion known
- Including asexuality when listing sexual orientations
- Educating LGBTQ+ club members on the asexual spectrum
- Allowing people to change their labels
- Making no assumptions

WAYS TO ENSURE ACE INCLUSION

MAKE YOUR INCLUSION KNOWN

Be explicit in including aces in your space, both so that aces know that they are welcome, and so that other club members know that aces must be included. Even though most LGBTQ+ youth have experienced discrimination and isolation themselves, some still do not readily accept aces; therefore, making your support and the club's support of ace identified students explicitly known from day one is vital in ensuring a safe space for ace members.

Make sure that you stop all acephobic behavior and comments that occur in your space, and ask the teachers that are involved in your LGBTQ+ club to do the same.

> To make your ace inclusion visible, consider hanging an ace inclusion poster in your LGBTQ+ club meeting space. We've included one in this kit to help you out, and more can always be ordered from http://schools.asexualoutreach.org/resources/

Ways to Ensure Ace Inclusion

INCLUDE ASEXUALITY WHEN LISTING SEXUAL ORIENTATIONS

There are numerous variations of the the LGBTQ+ acronym that you could use, and no acronym will ever be perfect. However, if you ever find yourself listing sexual orientations, ensure that you do not skip over asexuality. By including the asexual spectrum in your list, you are restating your support for aces, and you could potentially lead aces in your school to discover that their orientation has a label and that there is a community of people like them.

...PSSST!

Many organizations include "A" in their LGBTQ+ acronym, but unfortunately only use "A" to represent allies. If your "A" includes allies, make sure that it also includes asexuality (and possibly also aromantic and agender!)

Consider prompting discussion by proposing one of the following alternatives to the LGBTQ+ acronym. You may even find that one of these works better for your club!

- ☐ **GSM:** Gender and Sexual Minorities
- ☐ **GSRM:** Gender, Sexual, and Romantic Minorities
- ☐ **GSD:** Gender and Sexual Diversity
- ☐ **QUILTBAG:** "Queer/Questioning, Undecided, Intersex, Lesbian, Trans, Bisexual, Asexual, Gay/Genderqueer
- ☐ **MOGAI:** Marginalized Orientations, Gender Alignments, and Intersex

Ways to Ensure Ace Inclusion

EDUCATE LGBTQ+ CLUB MEMBERS ON THE ASEXUAL SPECTRUM

Without knowledge of the asexual spectrum, members of your LGBTQ+ club may be skeptical of or may react poorly to aces joining the group. In order to avoid backlash and harmful reactions, ensure that others in your club know about the asexual spectrum. If you do encounter negative reactions, firmly stand in support of aces – especially if there are aces present. It can be very difficult to defend one's identity against attackers, so make sure to explicitly defend aces that come under scrutiny in your group.

> Educating about the asexual spectrum could be as simple as prompting a discussion, though you can find more ideas and activities nearer the end of this chapter or at http://schools.asexualoutreach.org/activities/

ALLOW PEOPLE TO CHANGE THEIR LABELS

Coming to identify as ace can be a challenging process because it can be very difficult for aces to understand what sexual attraction actually is – especially if they do not experience it themselves. To help ease this process and to help lessen the confusion that many LGBTQ+ youth face, ensure that your LGBTQ+ club is a safe space for people to change labels. In many cases, people can cycle through orientation labels before they discover what best suits them, and this should be accepted.

Ways to Ensure Ace Inclusion

MAKE NO ASSUMPTIONS

Do not assume that people are interested in sex, that they have partners, or that they are interested in romantic relationships. Recognize that not everyone has "crushes" and that not everyone is inherently sexually/romantically interested in others. Additionally, do not assume that someone is not interested in romantic relationships or that they do not have "crushes" just because they are ace. There is a wide diversity of romanticism among aces, and an ace's sexual orientation does not determine anything about their romantic
orientation or involvement.

Do not make sexuality a requirement – understand that some people do not experience sexual attraction and that some do not desire sexual intimacy. This does not make someone a "prude" or "frigid"; it simply means that they experience attraction and desire differently than others, and that is okay.

Do not assume that aces are immature because they may not experience sexual attraction and may not desire sex. Sexual interest and activity are not equivalent to maturity, and so an ace's lack of sexual interest does not determine their maturity.

Finally, avoid making generalizations. Statements such as "everyone wants sex", or "everyone experiences/will eventually experience attraction to others" are not only incorrect, but can also be harmful and alienating to aces in your group.

> There may be aces in your club or meeting space without you even realizing it, and so in addition to being generally harmful, negative comments about the asexual spectrum may be especially harmful to those aces that aren't "out." In order to help prevent unintended oppression, act as though there are always aces present.

SUPPORTING ACES WHO JOIN YOUR CLUB

Because of the lack of support services for aces and because many aces consider themselves to fall under the LGBTQ+ umbrella, your LGBTQ+ club will likely be the first place that many aces in your school will go. Thus, making your club ace friendly can be instrumental in changing and bettering the lives of aces in your school and community.

In order to best support aces who come to your LGBTQ+ club, you must understand the issues that aces face and be willing to welcome and provide a supportive environment for them.

A detailed explanation of these issues can be found in *"An Introduction to the Asexual Spectrum"* in the first chapter of this book; however, the next page covers them briefly.

Supporting Aces who Join Your Club

ISSUES ACES IN YOUR GROUP MAY FACE

Aces are frequently victims of homophobia, transphobia, and other forms of oppression. They are more likely to be victims of bullying than cisgender straight youth, and school staff members are often ill-equipped to handle these oppressions. Respect that these oppression are real and harmful, regardless of an ace's identity.

Aces may have a difficult time accepting an ace identity because of societal stigmas and norms. Coming to identify as ace can additionally be a difficult process because it can be very difficult for aces to understand what sexual attraction actually is – especially if they do not experience it themselves.

Finally, an ace's parents, family, and peers may not support them or accept/understand their identity, and this may leave them with few options for finding support.

Supporting Aces who Join Your Club

PROVIDING RESOURCES, CONTACTS, AND SUPPORT

You may be in a position to directly support aces, and that could greatly benefit ace members of your group. Like when supporting any other student, if an ace brings up issues that they are facing, actively listen to them and accept those issues as legitimate regardless of your opinion of them. Let aces know which teachers and guidance counselors understand the asexual spectrum and are willing to support ace students.

You may not be comfortable or know enough information to be a direct supporter. If this is the case, help aces in your group find resources that can better support them. These resources may include the http://schools.asexualoutreach.org/ website, local asexual support or meetup groups, or even the informational flyers included in this kit. Additionally, if there are teachers or guidance counselors at your school who know about and are supportive of the asexual spectrum, you can help by letting aces in your group know this information.

> To ensure teachers and counselors know about the asexual spectrum, you may have to provide them with resources yourself. You will find a chapters in this book directed specifically at educators and guidance counselors.
> If you run out of copies, you can find printable versions at http://school.asexualoutreach.org/guide/

Ace Inclusion Guide for High Schools

Ace Education and Inclusion Activities for Your Club

ACE EDUCATION AND INCLUSION ACTIVITIES FOR YOUR CLUB

While it may be difficult to run an activity on a topic that you aren't incredibly familiar with, there are ways to successfully educate about the asexual spectrum given limited knowledge.

One simple way to bring the asexual spectrum to the attention of your LGBTQ+ club members is to have a discussion on it, including gray-asexual identities.

Other potential discussion topics could include ace inclusivity and how your LGBTQ+ club could be more welcoming, as well as the types of attraction – a topic that is relevant and beneficial to everyone.

If someone asks a question in a discussion that you don't know the answer to, instead of speculating, consider consulting this book, searching for an answer on **http://schools.asexualoutreach.org/**, or contacting Asexual Outreach for an answer.

 For more discussion topics, and for more activities you can run with your club, visit **http://schools.asexualoutreach.org/activities/**

Ace Education and Inclusion Activities for Your Club

 Asexual Awareness Week is a week of asexual education, advocacy, and awareness typically held near the end of October. Check http://schools.asexualoutreach.org/awareness-week/ for this year's dates!

Consider hosting an ace activity/event during Asexual Awareness Week, or look into bringing in a guest speaker from the local community or from Asexual Outreach to give a workshop on ace awareness and inclusivity.

For a lower key activity, host a movie night where you can screen (A)sexual – a documentary about the asexual spectrum and asexual movement. For a more ambitious project, try running a school wide awareness campaign. This could be putting up posters, running ace education announcements for a week, or even hosting a school wide assembly with a guest speaker.

Asexual Outreach has a series of workshops with various workshops designed for small groups, for large presentations, for school staff, and for school boards. If you're looking for a presentation on a specific topic or just for a general 101 workshop, contact us at schools@asexualoutreach.org and we'll bring a presenter to your school!

For more ace activity ideas including games you can play with your LGBTQ+ club, check out
http://schools.asexualoutreach.org/activities/

Ace Inclusion Guide for High Schools

This Ace Inclusion Guide for High Schools is a part of *Asexual Outreach's* larger youth outreach programming. Further school resources, including a digital copy of this entire guide, can be found at ***http://schools.asexualoutreach.org/***
For additional help including aces in your school and classes or to bring a speaker to your school, you can contact us by email at ***schools@asexualoutreach.org*** or by phone *(toll-free)* at ***1-855-5-ASEXUAL (1-855-527-3982)***.

Creating An Ace-Friendly School

CHAPTER 3

This Ace Inclusion Guide for High Schools is a part of *Asexual Outreach's* larger youth outreach programming. Further school resources, including a digital copy of this entire guide, can be found at **http://schools.asexualoutreach.org/**
For additional help including aces in your school and classes or to bring a speaker to your school, you can contact us by email at **schools@asexualoutreach.org** or by phone *(toll-free)* at **1-855-5-ASEXUAL (1-855-527-3982)**.

INTRODUCTION

Making your LGBTQ+ club ace friendly is a great start to including aces at your school! Unfortunately though, because they are often still left out of LGBTQ+ spaces, aces in your school may not know that your club is ace friendly, or may even assume the opposite. This chapter introduces a number of ways that you can make your school more ace inclusive as a whole.

The following ten ways will be discussed throughout this chapter:

» **School Staff & Policies**
- *Provide Staff with Chapters From This Book*
- *Have Ace Content Included in Sexual Education Classes*
- *Have Aces Included in Anti-Bullying Policies at Your School*

» **Ace Events**
- *Host Asexual Awareness Week Activities*
- *Bring in a Guest Speaker*
- *Include Aces in LGBTQ+ Events, Activities, and Discussions*
- *Advertise Ace Events and Discussions School-Wide*

» **Awareness Materials**
- *Hang Ace Inclusive Posters in Your School*
- *Make Ace 101 Flyers Available to Students and Staff*
- *Include Ace Related Books in Your Library*

INTRODUCTION

SCHOOL STAFF & POLICIES

PROVIDE STAFF WITH CHAPTERS FROM THIS BOOK

Because the asexual spectrum still lacks widespread awareness, it is likely that many of the staff at your school have never heard of it, and those who have do not know how to be inclusive of aces.

This often results in aces being alienated and invalidated in class discussions and curricula and being unable to find adequate support to help them with the issues they face. By providing the staff at your school with information on how to include and understand aces, you can make your school into a more inclusive space overall.

There are chapters in this book specifically for educators, guidance counselors, and administrators. Feel free to photocopy these chapters from this book to distribute to your school staff, or, alternatively, find printable versions of these chapters at *http://schools.asexualoutreach.org/guide/*

 **Make sure to also give staff members a copy of "An Introduction to the Asexual Spectrum" from the beginning of this book.**

School Staff & Policies

HAVE ACE CONTENT INCLUDED IN SEXUAL EDUCATION CLASSES

If the asexual spectrum is not mentioned in classes about sexuality, especially if other orientations are mentioned, aces in those classes may feel invalidated, and may be led to question whether or not their orientation is real and valid.

On the contrary, if teachers do explicitly teach asexual spectrum materials, several benefits will result.

First, this will validate the identities of aces in that class – aces who probably do not often have their identities validated.

Second, this may allow aces in that class who feel confused, isolated, or broken due to their sexual orientation to discover a label and a community that they may have difficulty finding elsewhere. Without the introduction of ace content, many aces spend years of their lives feeling confused and often subhuman, and so offering the opportunity for them to discover that they are normal can be life changing.

Third, teaching ace content legitimizes asexuality as a real orientation, and so students in that class will be more likely to accept aces and will be less likely to bully, marginalize, and ostracize them.

School Staff & Policies

> If any teachers in your school teach sexual education, offer them a copy of chapter 7, "Including Aces in Sexual Education" found in this book.
>
> If an external organization teaches sexual education at your school and does not include ace content, get in touch with Asexual Outreach and we can work with them to help them update their curriculum.
>
> Otherwise, see if you can get in touch with the educators that your school brings in to provide them with these resources.

HAVE ACES INCLUDED IN ANTI-BULLYING POLICIES AT YOUR SCHOOL

As you have read in the "Issues Aces in Your School May Face" section of "An Introduction to the Asexual Spectrum", aces are at a heightened risk of being the victims of bullying compared to their cisgender straight peers. If your school's anti-bullying policy lists individual sexual orientations, try to get your school administration to add asexuality to the list.

This will not only prompt a discussion about ace-related bullying among school administrators and staff, but will also help validate the seriousness of ace-related bullying, leading staff to more carefully deal with cases of it, and encouraging aces at your school to seek help if they are being bullied.

School Staff & Policies

ACE EVENTS

 Asexual Awareness Week usually falls near the end of October. For dates on when AAW is happening next, visit http://schools.asexualoutreach.org/awareness-week

HOST ASEXUAL AWARENESS WEEK ACTIVITIES

Asexual Awareness Week is a week to celebrate and learn more about the asexual spectrum. This is the perfect time to host ace events, discussions, activities, and other programming. Not only will this give information to the student populace, this will help to make your school a more inclusive place for aces. These activities could include ace discussions in your LGBTQ+ club, an ace awareness and inclusivity assembly for your school, an ace film/documentary screening, or a guest speaker presentation.

 For information on how to successfully run these events, or for other event and activity ideas, visit http://schools.asexualoutreach.org/activities/

BRING IN A GUEST SPEAKER

Bringing in a guest speaker to talk to your LGBTQ+ club or to your entire school is a great way to increase awareness of the asexual spectrum and to make your school a more ace inclusive space. Asexual Outreach has a series of workshops with various workshops designed for small groups, for large presentations, for school staff, and for school boards.

If you're looking for a presentation on a specific topic, for a general 101 workshop, or for any other ace workshop/presentation, contact us by email at **schools@asexualoutreach.org** or by phone (toll-free) at **1-855-5-ASEXUAL (1-855-527-3982)** and we'll bring a presenter to your school!

Ace Events

INCLUDE ACES IN LGBTQ+ EVENTS, ACTIVITIES, AND DISCUSSIONS

Event planners often forget to make room for aces in their LGBTQ+ events, and this can often make these events uncomfortable or even hostile for ace attendees. In order to avoid this, make sure to consider how inclusive your event will be from the beginning. Consider bringing an ace at your school onto your planning team so that they can help you make the event inclusive, or contact Asexual Outreach for help in making your event more inclusive.

You can contact us by email at schools@asexualoutreach.org or by phone (toll-free) at 1-855-5-ASEXUAL (1-855-527-3982).

Here are some questions that you can ask yourself during event planning to help you include aces in your events:

- ☐ **Does this event assume that all people experience sexual attraction and desire?**
- ☐ **How will attendees know that this event is ace inclusive?**
- ☐ **Does this event force anyone to "out" themselves?**
- ☐ **Will aces who are not "out" feel comfortable and supported in this space, even if you do not know that they are in this space?**
- ☐ **Will the event leaders feel comfortable stopping acephobic behavior and comments?**

ADVERTISE ACE EVENTS AND DISCUSSIONS SCHOOL-WIDE

Aces in your school may not know that your LGBTQ+ club is ace friendly, and others may not even know that there is a word to describe what you're feeling. By widely advertising ace events and discussions, aces in your school will more easily find spaces where their experience is validated, and those questioning or discovering the label will be able to find a community that will embrace them.

When putting on ace specific events, promote them as such, and promote them across your school - not just in your LGBTQ+ club. Depending on the rules of your school, posters, flyers, and announcements may help increase your event's visibility as well as awareness of the asexual spectrum.

 Make sure to read Chapter Two - Including Aces in Your Club on how your club can best support aces and make your club an ace inclusive space.

Awareness Materials

AWARENESS MATERIALS

HANG ACE INCLUSIVE POSTERS IN YOUR SCHOOL

Posters are a great tool for spreading visibility of aces and the asexual spectrum. Posted where appropriate in your school, these not only give information but can also show that a space is ace inclusive.

If you're looking for inclusion, education, and awareness posters, you can find printable copies on our website, and can request that we send you copies by mail at
http://schools.asexualoutreach.org/resources/

Awareness Materials

MAKE ACE 101 FLYERS AVAILABLE TO STUDENTS AND STAFF

Fliers are a great way of spreading information - especially about the asexual spectrum. A number of Asexual Outreach's "Asexuality 101" flyers and "Issues Young Aces Face" flyers can be found in your resource kit, and are a great starting point for people to learn about the asexual spectrum! Make these flyers available at your LGBTQ+ club's meetings, at counselors offices, and anywhere else that may be relevant in your school so that students at your school have the opportunity to learn more about the asexual spectrum on their own time. These are an especially great tool if you don't feel comfortable or knowledgeable enough to discuss the asexual spectrum with others but still want to promote ace inclusivity at your school.

If you run out of flyers along the way, Asexual Outreach can always send you more - just visit
http://schools.asexualoutreach.org/resources/

Awareness Materials

INCLUDE ACE RELATED BOOKS IN YOUR LIBRARY

Having ace related literature in your school library is a great way for people to discover and learn about the asexual spectrum, and as an added bonus, many people feel more comfortable referring to published books than they do referring to the internet. Not only are there excellent educational books on the subject, there are also plenty of young adult books with openly stated ace characters.

For a suggested list of books to bring into your school library and for more information on how to do so, visit
http://schools.asexualoutreach.org/books/

This Ace Inclusion Guide for High Schools is a part of *Asexual Outreach*'s larger youth outreach programming. Further school resources, including a digital copy of this entire guide, can be found at ***http://schools.asexualoutreach.org/***
For additional help including aces in your school and classes or to bring a speaker to your school, you can contact us by email at ***schools@asexualoutreach.org*** or by phone *(toll-free)* at ***1-855-5-ASEXUAL (1-855-527-3982)***.

Ace Information and Resources for Educators

CHAPTER 4

This Ace Inclusion Guide for High Schools is a part of *Asexual Outreach*'s larger youth outreach programming. Further school resources, including a digital copy of this entire guide, can be found at **http://schools.asexualoutreach.org/**
For additional help including aces in your school and classes or to bring a speaker to your school, you can contact us by email at **schools@asexualoutreach.org** or by phone *(toll-free)* at **1-855-5-ASEXUAL (1-855-527-3982)**.

Introduction

This chapter will you as an educator understand ace students, support ace students, include aces in their curriculum, and use ace inclusive language.

Here are some steps that you can take to better support aces in your classroom and school:

- **Learn about the asexual spectrum and the issues that ace students may face.**
- **Read the stories of aces in high school to better understand them.**
- **Reflect on your biases and the biases that may be present in your curricula.**
- **Use inclusive language in your teaching - consider how your material may be alienating to aces.**
- **Contact Asexual Outreach and other organizations for help or to bring in speakers.**

This chapter will cover:

» **Recognizing Alienating Aspects of Your Curricula**

» **Using Ace Inclusive Language in Your Classroom**

» **Supporting Ace Students Who Seek Help**

> If you are not yet entirely familiar with the asexual spectrum, it is strongly recommended that you read "Understanding the Asexual Spectrum" found at the start of this book. If you do not have access to this section, you can find a printable version of it online at http://schools.asexualoutreach.org/guide/

Recognizing Alienating Aspects of Your Curricula

RECOGNIZING ALIENATING ASPECTS OF YOUR CURRICULA

Because society often ignores aces while overwhelmingly catering to those who experience frequent sexual attraction, many people do not recognize when they are alienating aces. This unfortunately often extends to school curricula, and so you may be teaching material that excludes aces in your classroom. Teaching materials that invalidate aces can further feelings of isolation and brokenness, adding to the issues that they may already face. In addition, non-inclusive materials can prevent other students in your classes from understanding and accepting the asexual spectrum.

Checking your materials for ace-inclusivity before presenting them can go a long way in ensuring that aces do not feel invalidated in your classroom. The following are several questions that can guide you when checking over curriculum, assignments, activities, or any other materials in your classroom.

Recognizing Alienating Aspects of Your Curricula

Are non-inclusive assumptions being made?

Do your materials assume that everyone has crushes, and that everyone wants to get married and have children? Do they assume that all relationships have a sexual component, or that romantic relationships are more important and more valuable than other types of intimate relationships? Do your materials assume that all relationships look the same or that there is only one way to correctly have a relationship?

Do you assume that no aces or other LGBTQ+ students are present in your classroom?

Do your materials assume that all aces are neurotypical, have no disabilities, have no hormonal conditions, and have never suffered abuse?

Are certain sexual orientations mentioned while asexuality is left out?

Do your materials talk about discrimination against gay people while leaving out people of other marginalized sexual orientations such as asexuality? Is "LGBT" written out as "lesbian, gay, bisexual, and transgender"?

What kind of language is being used?

Are words in your materials unnecessarily gendered? Do your materials use phrases like "girlfriend and boyfriend," "husband and wife," or "Mom and Dad" – implying that all relationships are heterosexual and follow normative relationship structures?

Recognizing Alienating Aspects of Your Curricula

Is sexual attraction or sexual activity normalized?

Do your materials incorrectly assert that everyone is interested in finding a partner, or that everyone desires sex? Is marriage made to be a requirement or ideal? Do your materials state that experiencing sexual attraction and engaging in sexual activity are normal, while failing to mention that not experiencing sexual attraction and not engaging in sexual activity are just as normal?

Are there universal statements that may not account for everyone?

Do your materials use words/phrases like "everyone" or "all people" to describe experiences that not everyone actually has? Do they include phrases like "when you decide to have sex with your partner" that imply that sexual activity is an inevitability?

Are topics presented in a way that invalidates aces?

Do your materials teach that sexual activity is a basic need (common in psychology) or that sexual reproduction is a primary goal for all people (common evolutionary science)?

> "...it felt so strange and uncomfortable taking psychology, and learning about Freudian psychology. The idea that sex was a basic drive of humans was irritating, as I had never once actually wanted to be with anyone."
> - Emma Kate

Recognizing Alienating Aspects of Your Curricula

Do materials ignore the diversity of the ace community?

Are all aces in your materials white, cisgender, and heteroromantic? Are they all neurotypical, have no disabilities, have no hormonal conditions, and have never suffered abuse?

If you've answered yes to any of the above, your materials may not as inclusive as they could be. These questions are just a starting point in your journey to include aces. Because different subjects and topics may relate differently to the asexual spectrum, some of the above questions may not apply to your teaching while other, more relevant, questions may need to be added to your list.

> If you're ever in doubt about whether material is inclusive or not, or if you recognize non-inclusive aspects of your materials but do not know how to correct them, guessing should not be your first option. Get in touch with local ace organizations, or contact Asexual Outreach, either through email at schools@asexualoutreach.org, or through our toll-free number: 1-855-5-ASEXUAL (1-855-527-3982)

Using Ace Inclusive Language in Your Classroom

Using Ace Inclusive Language in Your Classroom

MAKE NO ASSUMPTIONS

Do not assume that people are interested in sex, that they have partners, or that they are interested in romantic relationships. Recognize that not everyone has "crushes" and that not everyone is inherently sexually/romantically interested in others. Additionally, do not assume that someone is not interested in romantic relationships or that they do not have "crushes" just because they are ace. There is a wide diversity of romanticism among aces, and an ace's sexual orientation does not determine anything about their romantic orientation or involvement.

Do not make sexuality a requirement – understand that some people do not experience sexual attraction and that some do not desire sexual intimacy. This does not make someone a "prude" or "frigid"; it simply means that they experience attraction and desire differently than others, and that is okay.

Do not assume that aces are immature because they may not experience sexual attraction and may not desire sex. Sexual interest and activity are not equivalent to maturity, and so an ace's lack of sexual interest does not determine their maturity.

Finally, avoid making generalizations. Statements such as "everyone wants sex", or "everyone experiences/will eventually experience attraction to others" are not only incorrect, but can also be harmful and alienating to aces in your class.

> There may be aces in your classroom without you even realizing it, and so in addition to being generally harmful, negative comments about asexuality may be especially harmful to those aces that aren't "out." In order to help prevent unintended oppression, act as though there are always aces present.

SUPPORTING ACE STUDENTS WHO SEEK HELP

Because knowledge of the asexual spectrum is not yet widespread, young aces often lack support systems. Aces at your school may face invalidation from parents and peers, may be the victims of bullying, and may feel isolated and broken in a society that expects them to experience sexual attraction, and to desire and engage in sexual activity.

Ace students may seek help from you for a wide range of issues. They may be questioning their identity, or may be unsure as to how they can fit in with friends and peers. They may have recently come out to parents or teachers who invalidated their orientation, or who refuse to attempt to understand them. They may be facing bullying because of their lack of sexual attraction or because of their non-hetero romantic orientation or non-conforming gender presentation. They may have been victim to sexual assault or "corrective" rape because of their orientation.

The reasons they may seek help are incredibly diverse, and may all need to be handled differently. However, validating their identity and their experiences should be central to your support.

Supporting Ace Students Who Seek Help

In short, here are some things you should and should not do when supporting an ace student.

Do:

- Validate an ace's identity as is
- Include ace resources alongside other resources about sexuality
- Allow students to explore their identity, and allow them to change their labels

Do not:

- Encourage aces to try sexual activity
- Tell aces that they are too young to know that they are ace
- Imply that sexual attraction, sexual desire, and interest in sexual activity are universally natural
- Suggest causes for their ace identity
- Use potential causes as a way to invalidate their ace identity
- "Out" an ace to others without their permission

> All of these points are greatly expanded upon in the "Information and Resources for Guidance Counselors" chapter of this ace-inclusion guide. If you are looking to take a more invested role in supporting ace students at your school, attain a copy of that section and read through it!
> A printable version of that chapter can be found at
> http://schools.asexualoutreach.org/guide/

ⓘ This Ace Inclusion Guide for High Schools is a part of *Asexual Outreach's* larger youth outreach programming. Further school resources, including a digital copy of this entire guide, can be found at ***http://schools.asexualoutreach.org/***
For additional help including aces in your school and classes or to bring a speaker to your school, you can contact us by email at ***schools@asexualoutreach.org*** or by phone *(toll-free)* at ***1-855-5-ASEXUAL (1-855-527-3982)***.

# ACE Information and Resources for Guidance Counselors

CHAPTER 5

This Ace Inclusion Guide for High Schools is a part of *Asexual Outreach's* larger youth outreach programming. Further school resources, including a digital copy of this entire guide, can be found at **http://schools.asexualoutreach.org/**
For additional help including aces in your school and classes or to bring a speaker to your school, you can contact us by email at **schools@asexualoutreach.org** or by phone *(toll-free)* at **1-855-5-ASEXUAL (1-855-527-3982)**.

Introduction

Because knowledge of the asexual spectrum is not yet widespread, young aces often lack support systems. Aces at your school may face invalidation from parents and peers, may be the victims of bullying, and may feel isolated and broken in a society that expects them to experience sexual attraction and to desire and engage in sexual activity. In fact, all of these are common narratives among ace youth, and so as a guidance counselor, it is vital that you understand the asexual spectrum, the issues that aces face, and the things that you should and should not do while supporting them.

This chapter will outline some steps you can take to begin better supporting ace students at your school.

> 💡 If you are not yet entirely familiar with the asexual spectrum, it is strongly recommended that you read "Understanding the Asexual Spectrum" found at the start of this book. If you do not have access to this section, you can find a printable version of it online at **http://asexualoutreach.org/guide/**

Within counseling, there is a pervasive belief that sexuality is a healthy and often necessary component of intimate relationships while for many people, especially for many aces, this may not be the case.

Confronting Preconceived Notions

CONFRONTING PRECONCEIVED NOTIONS

In order to best help ace students seeking support, it is important to reflect on your own biases and challenge personal attitudes you may have. Consider answering the following questions:

Prior to receiving this resource, how much did you know about the asexual spectrum?

_____
_____
_____
_____

How much of your higher education and training has been focused on the asexual spectrum?

_____
_____
_____
_____

Confronting Preconceived Notions

What are your assumptions about asexuality?

_____
_____
_____
_____

Do you believe that sexual activity is necessary for true intimate relationships?

_____
_____
_____
_____

How well would you be able to support a student who states that they are ace?

_____
_____
_____
_____

Do you think that some students are too young to identify as ace?

_____
_____
_____
_____

SUPPORTING ACE STUDENTS WHO SEEK HELP

Ace students may seek help from you for a wide range of issues. They may be questioning their identity, or may be unsure as to how they can fit in with friends and peers. They may have recently come out to parents or teachers who invalidated their orientation, or who refuse to attempt to understand them. They may be facing bullying because of their lack of sexual attraction or because of their non-hetero romantic orientation or non-conforming gender presentation. They may have been the victim of sexual assault or "corrective" rape because of their orientation.

The reasons they may seek help are incredibly diverse, and may all need to be handled differently. However, validating their identity and their experiences should be central to your support.

Supporting Ace Students Who Seek Help

The following pages expand on the following things you should and should not do when supporting an ace student.

Do:

- Validate an ace's identity as is
- Allow students to explore their identity, and allow them to change their labels
- Include ace resources alongside other resources about sexuality

Do not:

- Encourage aces to try sexual activity
- Tell aces that they are too young to know that they are ace
- Imply that sexual attraction, sexual desire, and interest in sexual activity are universally natural
- Suggest causes for their ace identity
- Use potential causes as a way to invalidate their ace identity
- "Out" an ace to others without their permission
- Assert that an ace's partner has a right to sexual activity

Supporting Ace Students Who Seek Help

✓ Do validate an ace's identity as is.

Young aces are frequently invalidated by peers, parents, teachers, and society in general. Often this invalidation comes at a suggestion that the asexual spectrum doesn't exist, that an ace is too young to know their identity or that they have not found the right person yet. In other cases, people use an ace's disabilities, neurodivergency, hormonal levels, or past abuse as an excuse not to accept the aces identity, despite that these experiences do not invalidate an ace identity in any way.

It is essential that you do not invalidate any ace's identity, regardless of circumstance. In order to truly support aces, you must validate their identity as is, and must validate their identity despite criticism from parents or other staff.

✓ Do include ace resources alongside other resources about sexuality.

Because knowledge about the asexual spectrum is not yet widespread, it is possible that students in your school who would identify as ace do not even know that identifying as such is an option. Including ace resources alongside other sexuality resources can help ace youth to discover the asexual spectrum, preventing them from enduring years of feeling broken. Additionally, including ace resources will help students who already identify as ace to feel validated and supported. Finally, including these resources will help to normalize the asexual spectrum, encouraging z-sexual students at your school to better accept and include aces.

Supporting Ace Students Who Seek Help

✓ **Do allow students to explore their identity, and allow them to change their labels.**

Coming to identify as ace can be a challenging process because it can be very difficult for aces to understand what sexual attraction actually is – especially if they do not experience it themselves. Youth are often pressured to choose a label and stick with it, but this unnecessarily pressures them to conform to a narrow view of identity, and often pressures them to change themselves to better "fit" into a label. In addition, when youth do change their labels, others may distrust the validity of that person's identity, so it is essential that you validate and trust in how youth identify, even if this identity is not permanent.

✓ **Do consider the ways societal norms harm aces.**

Societal norms - especially compulsory sexuality (the pervasive belief that everyone experiences sexual attraction and that everyone can and should engage in sexual activity) - can actively harm aces. Although these norms may cause aces to be uncomfortable with their ace identity, the ace identity is not causing this discomfort itself.

If an ace is uncomfortable with their orientation, consider discussing these harmful societal expectations with them. Their orientation is not the cause of their discomfort, but rather, harmful societal norms are the cause. Explore this distinction with them, and then work with the ace to help them understand how they can still live a fulfilling and enjoyable life, despite these discomforting societal norms.

Supporting Ace Students Who Seek Help

✘ Do *not* encourage aces to try sexual activity.

Sexual orientation is based on who a person is sexually attracted to, not what sexual behaviours a person has. Encouraging an ace to "try" sexual activity to either confirm or refute their ace identity is one of the worst approaches you can take in regards to supporting ace students. Aces are already heavily pressured into sexual activity as a result of compulsory sexuality; if you add to this pressure by encouraging them to try sexual activity, this could lead to sexual assault and/or rape. Instead, the better approach would be to validate the ace's identity and to assure them that there are no prerequisites for identifying as ace.

✘ Do *not* suggest causes for their ace identity or use potential causes as a way to invalidate their ace identity.

There is no one way that people come to an ace identity, and while some people may feel like they were always asexual, some people come to their ace identity through other experiences. Many aces have disabilities, are neurodivergent, have hormonal conditions, and/or have survived sexual assault. Some aces come to identify with the asexual spectrum via these experiences, and this does not make their identity any less valid than any other sexual identity.

It is never a good idea to attempt to "cure" an ace's sexuality, even if there appears to be an identifiable "cause" to their orientation. If an ace is comfortable with and not distressed by their orientation, there is certainly no reason to attempt to change that. If, alternatively, an ace is not comfortable with their orientation, recognize that that discomfort may be the result of incompatible societal expectations or ostracization from peers.

Supporting Ace Students Who Seek Help

✖ Do not imply that sexual attraction, sexual desire, and interest in sexual activity are universally natural.

Many people assume that experiencing sexual attraction, sexual desire, and interest in sexual activity are better than their not experiencing these. On a larger scale, society is often set up to favor people who experience all of these above those who do not. However, not experiencing sexual desire, sexual attraction, and interest in sexual activity are not lesser; they are simply different experiences. Implying that these experiences are universally natural can greatly harm aces.

Instead, you should try to explain that diverse experiences do not follow a hierarchy, and that no experiences are inherently better. Alternatively, if you must state that experiencing the above is natural, also make sure to state that not experiencing the above is equally natural.

✖ Do not tell aces that they are too young to know that they are ace.

Ace youth are commonly told that they are "too young" to know that they are ace, that they will "grow out of it" or that they are a "late bloomer". These dismissive comments are not helpful to aces - in fact, they further the invalidation and lack of support that many young aces already experience. It may be the case that an ace will eventually identify with another orientation; given the fluidity of sexuality, that does happen. However, it is important that youth feel validated in their current identity. You will do far more damage in telling an ace that they will eventually change then you would by not telling the same to someone who will eventually change.

Supporting Ace Students Who Seek Help

✖ Do *not* "out" an ace to others without their permission.

Many aces are not comfortable being "out" to others (ie. revealing their sexual orientation to others), and so "outing" them without their permission can be very damaging. Aces may be especially uncomfortable with their parents knowing their orientation, so it is important that you do not discuss the student's identity with their parents without first receiving permission from them.

✖ Do *not* assert that an ace's partner has a right to sexual activity.

Students who are in a relationship may seek help from you because one student wants less sexual activity than the other. (This is especially common where one partner is ace and the other is not.) While these differing levels of interest in sexual activity may be causing issues in the relationship, you must not attempt to resolve these issues by encouraging an ace student to have more sex. It is not an ace's job to provide sex for their partner, and if any person does not what to have sex for any reason, that must be respected. If a person is pressured into having sex to appease their partner, this is sexual assault and should not be taken lightly.

What you should do instead is encourage open communication within the relationship. You can explore the cause of sexual incompatibilities with these students, but you should always side with any student who does not want sex.

Supporting Ace Students Who Seek Help

Additionally, you should discuss consent and sexual coercion with students to ensure that they know that they never have to have sex if they do not want to, and that they should not expect sex and must not pressure their partner into having sex.

> "I figured out I was asexual with a girlfriend in high school. She was really overly sexual, and wanted me to do a lot more stuff than I was really into. She was abusive and emotionally manipulative, and I was afraid of her, so I consented, and I tried to make it seem like I was into it, although I was not... I thought it was kinda gross, honestly. It also caused me dysphoria in a way that is a little hard to explain. The trans aspect really just made it terribly unpleasant to have to do anything remotely sexual. It wasn't just that I was not into it, I couldn't deal with it. It made me sad."
> — Anonymous

This Ace Inclusion Guide for High Schools is a part of *Asexual Outreach's* larger youth outreach programming. Further school resources, including a digital copy of this entire guide, can be found at
http://schools.asexualoutreach.org/
For additional help including aces in your school and classes or to bring a speaker to your school, you can contact us by email at
schools@asexualoutreach.org or by phone *(toll-free)* at
1-855-5-ASEXUAL (1-855-527-3982).

Ace Information and Resources for Administrators

CHAPTER 6

This Ace Inclusion Guide for High Schools is a part of *Asexual Outreach*'s larger youth outreach programming. Further school resources, including a digital copy of this entire guide, can be found at **http://schools.asexualoutreach.org/**
For additional help including aces in your school and classes or to bring a speaker to your school, you can contact us by email at **schools@asexualoutreach.org** or by phone *(toll-free)* at **1-855-5-ASEXUAL (1-855-527-3982)**.

Introduction

Aces are at an elevated risk of being the victims of bullying and harassment, are often alienated in classrooms where educators do not understand the asexual spectrum, and are frequently invalidated in sexual education classes. These issues can be mitigated by ensuring that staff at your school understand the asexual spectrum, by including aces in your school's anti-bullying policies and procedures, and by requiring that sexual education is ace-inclusive.

This chapter will help you more comprehensively understand these issues and the damage they cause, and will expand on the following five actions that you can take to lessen this damage:

» **Challenge your own preconceived ideas about sexuality.**

» **Require the inclusion of asexual-spectrum content in sexual education classes at your school.**

» **Include asexuality in anti-bullying policies at your school, and ensure that staff are educated in dealing with ace-related bullying.**

» **Support and participate in ace awareness and education activities/campaigns.**

» **Bring in a presenter to give a workshop to your staff on ace-inclusivity.**

> ⚡ **PSSST...**
> If you are not yet entirely familiar with the asexual spectrum, it is strongly recommended that you read "An Introduction to the Asexual Spectrum" found at the start of this book. If you do not have access to this section, you can find a printable version of it online at
> http://schools.asexualoutreach.org/guide/

Confronting Preconceived Notions

CONFRONTING PRECONCEIVED NOTIONS

In order to better include aces in your school, it is important to reflect on your own biases and challenge personal attitudes you may have. Consider answering the following questions:

Prior to receiving this resource, how much did you know about the asexual spectrum?

_____
_____
_____
_____

How much of your higher education and training has been focused on the asexual spectrum?

_____
_____
_____
_____

What are your assumptions about asexuality?

_____
_____
_____
_____

Confronting Preconceived Notions

Do you believe that sexual activity is necessary for true intimate relationships?
_____
_____
_____
_____

How well would you be able to support a student who states that they are ace?
_____
_____
_____
_____

Do you think that some students are too young to identify as ace?
_____
_____
_____
_____

Confronting Preconceived Notions

REQUIRE THE INCLUSION OF ASEXUAL-SPECTRUM CONTENT IN SEXUAL EDUCATION CLASSES AT YOUR SCHOOL

Including the asexual spectrum in sexual education classes is incredibly important for the wellbeing of ace students for a number of reasons. If the asexual spectrum is not mentioned in classes about sexuality, especially if other orientations are mentioned, aces in those classes may feel invalidated, and may be led to question whether or not their orientation is real and valid.

On the contrary, if asexual spectrum content is explicitly taught, several benefits will result.

First, this will validate the identities of aces sexual education classes – aces who probably do not often have their identities validated.

Second, this may allow aces those classes who feel confused, isolated, or broken due to their sexual orientation to discover a label and a community that they may have difficulty finding elsewhere. Without the introduction of ace content, many aces spend years of their lives feeling confused and often subhuman, and so offering the opportunity for them to discover that they are normal can be life changing.

Third, teaching ace content legitimizes asexuality as a real orientation, and so students in those classes will be more likely to accept aces and will be less likely to bully, marginalize, and ostracize them.

Confronting Preconceived Notions

Included in this book is a chapter for ensuring inclusive sexual education. If any educators at your school teach sexual education classes, ensure that they read this chapter so that they know how to best include aces in their teaching.

If your school brings in an external organization or presenter to teach sexual education, inquire about their inclusion of aces in their teaching. If they do not currently include aces or are unsure how to include aces, offer them a copy of the aforementioned chapter, or connect them with Asexual Outreach to help them introduce this vital content into their materials.

Finally, consider contacting **Asexual Outreach** to have an ace-inclusion workshop presented to the sexual educators at your school.

You can contact us by email at schools@asexualoutreach.org or by phone (toll-free) at 1-855-5-ASEXUAL (1-855-527-3982).

Confronting Preconceived Notions

INCLUDE ASEXUALITY IN ANTI-BULLYING POLICIES AT YOUR SCHOOL, AND ENSURE THAT STAFF ARE EDUCATED IN DEALING WITH ACE-RELATED BULLYING

Young aces are at a heightened risk of being the victims of bullying compared to their cisgender straight peers, yet schools often lack the tools and resources to deal with ace related bullying. Because many aces have LGBQ+ romantic orientations and/or are aromantic, many are trans and/or non-binary, and many present their gender in non-conventional ways, many young aces are the victims of homophobic and transphobic bullying.

Further still, many young aces are bullied just for being different. They are often called prudes, frigid, and other names/descriptors in an attempt to harm them, and these certainly can be harmful.

In more drastic cases, they may be physically and sexually assaulted, and in some cases can be victims of "corrective" rape.

Ace related bullying might not always be obvious; because not everyone understands the asexual spectrum, many people fail to recognize acephobic bullying. Furthermore, because ace related bullying is not always treated seriously, because aces may not wish to be outed, and because of the shaming inherent in this bullying, this bullying often goes unreported.

Confronting Preconceived Notions

Acephobic bullying is a serious matter, and it likely affects many students in your school. Despite the often elusive nature of this bullying, there are actions that you can take as an administrator to reduce its damaging effects.

To begin, ensure that the educators and staff at your school understand the asexual spectrum as well as acephobic bullying. For school staff, simply knowing about the existence of the asexual spectrum and ace-related bullying can encourage them to take this bullying more seriously and can help them to identify and stop instances of it.

> Along with containing a comprehensive overview of the asexual spectrum, this ace inclusion book contains specific chapters targeted directly at educators and guidance counselors. You are encouraged to copy these sections from the information guide and distribute them to staff members at your school. If you do not have access to the guide itself, you can find printable versions of each chapter at **http://schools.asexualoutreach.org/guide/**

Additionally, if your school's anti-bullying policy lists individual sexual orientations, work to include asexuality on the list. This will not only prompt a discussion about ace-related bullying among your fellow school administrators and staff, but will also help validate the seriousness of ace-related bullying, leading staff to more carefully deal with cases of it, and encouraging aces at your school to seek help if they are being bullied.

Confronting Preconceived Notions

SUPPORT AND PARTICIPATE IN ACE AWARENESS AND EDUCATION ACTIVITIES/CAMPAIGNS

If students or clubs in your school plan ace activities or campaigns, make sure to offer your support to them. Some students may assume that you do not understand or support aces, and so assuring them of your support could help them feel more comfortable in running ace activities and campaigns. If students are looking to advertise their initiatives in your school, whether through posters, your school's PA system, or any other means, allow them to do so!

If parents or others in your community are concerned about your open support of the asexual spectrum, make sure to solidly affirm your position to them, and offer them ace resources to explain why your support is necessary. Aces need to be explicitly supported on a school wide level, and parental opinions or concerns must not trump the safety and wellbeing of aces at your school and in your community.

Confronting Preconceived Notions

BRING IN A PRESENTER TO GIVE A WORKSHOP TO YOUR STAFF ON ACE-INCLUSIVITY

Even with the resources provided in this book, educators and other staff at your school may not fully understand the asexual spectrum or the issues that aces at your school may face, and many may not take the initiative to find supplementary resources to help them better understand. Other staff may disregard the resources in this book, or may have specific questions that this book does not address. Further still, you may simply feel that written resources are not the most effective way to communicate these resources to your staff.

A potential solution to any of the above could be to bring in an ace activist to present a workshop for your staff. Asexual Outreach has a series of school workshops that target a variety of audiences including students, staff, parents, and school boards, and can often bring presenters to your school for free or for minimal cost.

> Get in contact with us if you are interested in bringing in a presenter to your school. You can reach us by email at **schools@asexualoutreach.org** or by phone (toll-free) at **1-855-5-ASEXUAL (1-855-527-3982)**.

ℹ️ This Ace Inclusion Guide for High Schools is a part of *Asexual Outreach's* larger youth outreach programming. Further school resources, including a digital copy of this entire guide, can be found at ***http://schools.asexualoutreach.org/***
For additional help including aces in your school and classes or to bring a speaker to your school, you can contact us by email at ***schools@asexualoutreach.org*** or by phone *(toll-free)* at ***1-855-5-ASEXUAL (1-855-527-3982)***.

ACE-INCLUSIVE SEXUAL EDUCATION

CHAPTER 7

> This Ace Inclusion Guide for High Schools is a part of *Asexual Outreach's* larger youth outreach programming. Further school resources, including a digital copy of this entire guide, can be found at ***http://schools.asexualoutreach.org/***
> For additional help including aces in your school and classes or to bring a speaker to your school, you can contact us by email at ***schools@asexualoutreach.org*** or by phone *(toll-free)* at ***1-855-5-ASEXUAL (1-855-527-3982)***.

INTRODUCTION

Including the asexual spectrum in sexual education classes is incredibly important for the wellbeing of ace students for a number of reasons If the asexual spectrum is not mentioned in classes about sexuality, especially if other orientations are mentioned, aces in your class may feel invalidated, and may be led to question whether or not their orientation is real and valid. On the contrary, if you do explicitly teach asexual spectrum content, several benefits will result.

First, this will validate the identities of aces in your class – aces who probably do not often have their identities validated.

Second, this may allow aces in your class who feel confused, isolated, or broken due to their sexual orientation to discover a label and a community that they may have difficulty finding elsewhere. Without the introduction of ace content, many aces spend years of their lives feeling confused and often subhuman, and so offering the opportunity for them to discover that they are normal can be life changing.

Third, teaching ace content legitimizes asexuality as a real orientation, and so students in your class will be more likely to accept aces and will be less likely to bully, marginalize, and ostracize them.

This chapter will help you understand the asexual spectrum, the issues that aces in your class may face, and the ways that you can include aces in your classes, so that you can better understand and support ace students in your classroom.

INTRODUCTION

> "In school, sex-ed lessons are pretty awful, because there's always that one person saying "It's natural, why are you disgusted by it?", and you can't offer an explanation when you don't understand why you feel that way yourself and the teacher never covers asexuality.
>
> There's also the lesson where you're forced into practising putting a condom on a polystyrene genital. It made me feel incredibly uncomfortable and it's totally irrelevant to me (since I would only ever have sex if I wanted to have kids, since I'm repulsed)."
> - Sarah

> "...without proper education regarding asexuality and others I was in a sexually abusive relationship because I was told "it's love" even when I didn't have that attraction. I thought I was broken. 4 years later I still deal with the trauma."
> - Anonymous

INTRODUCTION

This chapter will help you as a sex educator understand ace students, support ace students, include aces in their curriculum, and use ace inclusive language. Here are some steps that you can take to better support aces in your classroom and school:

- Learn about the asexual spectrum and the issues that ace students may face.
- Read the stories of aces in high school to better understand them.
- Reflect on your biases and the biases that may be present in your curriculum.
- Use inclusive language in your teaching - consider how your material may be alienating to aces.
- Educate about the asexual spectrum and teach sexuality as a spectrum.

Contact **Asexual Outreach** and other organizations for help or to bring in speakers.

> If you are not yet entirely familiar with the asexual spectrum, it is strongly recommended that you read "An Introduction to the Asexual Spectrum" found at the start of this book. If you do not have access to this section, you can find a printable version of it online at **http://schools.asexualoutreach.org/guide/**

This chapter will cover:

» **Reflect on Your Own Biases**
» **Using Ace Inclusive Language**
» **Educating About the Asexual Spectrum**

REFLECTING ON YOUR OWN BIASES

In order to best include aces in your teaching, it is important to reflect on your own biases and challenge personal attitudes you may have.

Consider answering the following questions:

Prior to receiving this resource, how much did you know about the asexual spectrum?

_____
_____
_____
_____

How much of your higher education and training has been focused on the asexual spectrum?

_____
_____
_____
_____

What are your assumptions about asexuality?

_____
_____
_____
_____

Reflecting on Your Own Biases

Do you believe that sexual relations are necessary for true intimate relationships?

_____
_____
_____
_____

How well would you be able to support a student who states that they are ace?

_____
_____
_____
_____

Do you think that some students are too young to identify as ace?

_____
_____
_____
_____

Reflecting on Your Own Biases

USING ACE INCLUSIVE LANGUAGE

Because sexual relationships and sexual attraction are highly normalized in our society, it is incredibly easy for people to unintentionally and unknowingly make statements that alienate aces. When taught inclusively, sexual education classes can help many students feel validated in their orientations and experiences; on the contrary, if sex educators are not careful to use inclusive language, sexual education classes can be very invalidating to some students.

The following are five examples of common statements that do not entirely include aces. Take a minute to write out how you think each statement might alienate aces in your classroom. Then, take a look at the next pages to learn the issues with each statement and the ways you can make these statements more inclusive.

1. "As puberty begins, all of you will start taking interest in others. You will all eventually develop sexual urges toward others, and this is completely normal."

_____
_____
_____
_____

2. "When you decide to have sex with a partner, make sure that you are having sex safely."

_____
_____
_____
_____

Reflecting on Your Own Biases

3. "Sex is a good thing, and there is no shame in having as many sexual partners as you wish."

_____
_____
_____
_____

4. "Because all of you will eventually have sex, it is important to know how to protect yourself from unwanted STD's/STI's."

_____
_____
_____
_____

5. "Some boys like girls. Some girls like boys. Some boys like boys, and some girls like girls. Some boys and girls like both boys and girls."

_____
_____
_____
_____

Issues With These Statements and Their Solutions

ISSUES WITH THESE STATEMENTS AND THEIR SOLUTIONS

1. "As puberty begins, all of you will start taking interest in others. You will all eventually develop sexual urges toward others, and this is completely normal."

This statement tells students that everyone experiences sexual attraction once they reach a certain age or developmental period. Effectively, this tells students that the asexual spectrum does not exist.

Aces in your classroom who do not know about the asexual spectrum may be led to believe that they are a late bloomer, and may continue waiting for years for sexuality to develop. Many teenage aces who do not know about the asexual spectrum believe that they are "broken" and non-inclusive sexual education might even encourage them to feel this way. Additionally, peers may also assume that there is something wrong with aces, and may subsequently isolate or bully them.

The following is an inclusive alternative to the above statement:

> "As puberty begins, you may start taking interest in others. You may develop sexual urges toward others, or you may not. Both are completely normal."

Issues With These Statements and Their Solutions

2. "When you decide to have sex with a partner, make sure that you are having sex safely."

This statement implies that sex is an inevitability - that all people will eventually have sex, and possibly that all partners will eventually have sex with one another. This statement may alienate aces that are not interested in having sex and aces that are sex-repulsed.

Additionally, it teaches students that they can expect sex in a relationship, and that all of their partners will eventually have sex with them if they wait long enough or pressure them enough. This can be dangerous to all students, and can possibly lead to sexual assault and rape.

It is essential to highlight that students always have a choice not to have sex. This can be as simple as replacing the word "when" with "if" in relevant statements. The following example applies this to the above statement:

"If you decide to have sex with a partner, make sure that you are having sex safely."

Issues With These Statements and Their Solutions

3. "Sex is a good thing, and there is no shame in having as many sexual partners as you wish."

There are two issues with this statement. The first is that sex is not inherently a good thing. It can be positive in many instances, but it can be very negative, and can also be neither positive nor negative.

Telling students that sex is a good thing may lead them to disregard the damage that comes with sexual assault and rape. This may make students less likely to respect when others say "no" or do not explicitly consent, and may make students believe that it is not entirely okay to say "no".

This may make students who do not want to have sex feel that there is something wrong with them, and could further contribute to aces' feelings of "brokenness."

The second issue with this statement is that it does not make clear that there is also no shame in having as few sexual partners as one wishes, including no sexual partners. Only noting that it is okay to have as many sexual partners as one wants again elevates sexual activity to a harmful ideal.

To fix both of these issues, consider the following rephrasing:

> "Sex can be a good thing, but it is not always a good thing, and it is not a good thing for everyone. There is no shame in having as many sexual partners as you wish, but there is also no shame in having as few sexual partners as you wish - including no sexual partners at all."

Issues With These Statements and Their Solutions

4. "Because all of you will eventually have sex, it is important to know how to protect yourself from unwanted STD's/STI's."

Like the first statement, this statement tells students that everyone will eventually have sex, and this is not necessarily the case - especially among aces. Consider the following rephrasing:

> "Because some of you may eventually have sex, it is important to know how to protect yourself from unwanted STD's/STI's."

5. "Some boys like girls. Some girls like boys. Some boys like boys, and some girls like girls. Some boys and girls like both boys and girls."

This statement suggests that everyone experiences attraction - whether that be sexual or romantic attraction. Of course, this is not the case, and so in order to prevent alienating students and invalidating the asexual spectrum, it should be noted that some people are not sexually and/or romantically interested in others.

A second issue with this statement is that it ignores non-binary genders and sexes, and ignores all sexual orientations other than heterosexual, homosexual, and bisexual.

The following is an example rephrasing:

> "Some people like other people of the same gender, some people like other people of another gender, some people like other people of multiple genders, and some people do not like others at all.

EDUCATING ABOUT THE ASEXUAL SPECTRUM

There is no single correct way to include the asexual spectrum in your classes and curricula, and different situations often call for different approaches.

In this section, a number of best practices will be introduced to get you started in including ace content in your teaching.

These include:

- *Teaching sexuality as a spectrum*
- *Separating sex and romance*
- *Redefining sex positivity to include aces*
- *Highlighting consent in your teaching*

TEACHING SEXUALITY AS A SPECTRUM

Teaching about the asexual spectrum does not necessarily have to mean listing off all of the possible orientations that fall along it. In fact, listing off orientations is often not the best way to start teaching others about the asexual spectrum, as the amount of information presented can be excessive, and as students may be further alienated if you miss including their orientation or experience. Even though labels are important to a lot of people, they are certainly limited and can not comprehensively match anyone's experience.

A better way to teach about the asexual spectrum and about sexuality in general is to discuss the wide diversity of attractions, desires, and experiences. Teach about the different types of attraction – especially about sexual and romantic attraction – and teach that these attractions are spectrums and that these attractions are not always concurrent and do not always align with one another. In addition to teaching that the target genders of these attractions greatly vary, teach that levels of attraction also vary and that some do not experience these attractions at all.

Finally, ensure your students know that everyone's experience of attraction and desire is different, and that – importantly – everyone's experiences are valid.

Educating About the Asexual Spectrum

SEPARATING SEX AND ROMANCE

It is important to note that romance and love do not always equate to sex. Teaching youth that the two concepts can be independent can lead to less confusion and self-invalidation if they enter into intimate relationships. By separating sex and romance, individuals will be more able to explore feelings and emotions for their partners more comfortably and with less pressure for sexual activity that they may not want, that they may be uncomfortable with, or that they may lack interest in.

Societal norms often hold that sexual activity is a necessary component and an eventuality of intimate relationships, and this can unnecessarily pressure people into sexual activity. In fact, there is no single form or direction that a relationship can or should take; in reality, relationships are complex and can incorporate any combination of sexual, romantic, platonic, sensual, and emotional elements, and all of these combinations are equally valid. Teaching that all relationships are different and that they do not need to incorporate sexual activity, nor do they need to incorporate any of the above elements can benefit all students.

Educating About the Asexual Spectrum

REDEFINING SEX POSITIVITY TO INCLUDE ACES

It is becoming more and more popular to teach sexual education in a sex-positive manner. Conventional sex-positivity promotes sexual activity as fundamentally uplifting, healthy, and pleasurable, and encourages sexual activity as long as it is consensual and safe. While sexuality can be healthy, and while people should be able to engage in consensual sex as often as they wish, most fail to note that people should be able to engage in sex as infrequently as they want, even if that means not having sex at all. Conventional sex-positivity may not resonate well with aces in your class, as it often promotes sexual activity as the ideal.

If you are teaching from a sex-positive perspective, it is essential that you do not forget that sexual activity is not always positive, and that not everybody desires it. Sexual activity can be deeply damaging in some cases, and that should be recognized and validated. In addition, some people have no interest in sex, and some find it to be neither positive nor negative. Choice is a key component of sex positivity, and the choice to not have sex should not be diminished as lesser.

Along similar lines, many people assume that abstinence is always a result of societal repression - usually at the hand of deeply held religious belief. Some further believe that people need to be "liberated" from their abstinence or the reasons that led to it. This is not only damaging to a lot of aces who do not wish to have sex, but can be damaging to anyone of any sexuality who wishes not to have sex. Abstinence is okay, regardless of reasoning.

Educating About the Asexual Spectrum

HIGHLIGHTING CONSENT IN YOUR TEACHING

Explicitly discussing consent and the aspects therein are vitally important. Because intimate relationships are often expected to be sexual, many people face significant pressure to introduce a sexual component into their relationships. Many people believe that gaining consent from a partner is as simple as them agreeing to participate in sexual activity; however, if a person was pressured or coerced into agreeing, this is not consent. Saying "no" to sexual activity can be especially difficult for youth who are striving to fit in, and can be additionally difficult for aces who feel broken as a result of their lack of sexual attraction, and thus assume that there is something wrong with them for not wanting sex.

Because of the pervasive societal belief that everyone experiences sexual attraction and that everyone can and should engage in sexual activity - a phenomenon known as compulsory sexuality - many are lead to believe that there is something wrong with people who are not engaging in sexual activities or who are in relationships without sexual activities. As some aces are not interested in engaging in sexual activities, compulsory sexuality can leave aces feeling like they are not fulfilling relationship expectations. This can pressure aces into engaging in unwanted and undesired sexual acts. If a person is not comfortable with the sexual acts that they are pressured into participating in, this is sexual assault and should not be taken lightly. Nobody should make others feel inadequate for not wanting to participate in sexual activities, yet this is common in partnerships where one person is ace and the other is not. Consent and communication is vital in all relationships regardless of participants' orientations.

Educating About the Asexual Spectrum

ⓘ This Ace Inclusion Guide for High Schools is a part of *Asexual Outreach's* larger youth outreach programming. Further school resources, including a digital copy of this entire guide, can be found at
http://schools.asexualoutreach.org/
For additional help including aces in your school and classes or to bring a speaker to your school, you can contact us by email at ***schools@asexualoutreach.org*** or by phone *(toll-free)* at
1-855-5-ASEXUAL (1-855-527-3982).

Glossary

CHAPTER 8

This Ace Inclusion Guide for High Schools is a part of *Asexual Outreach's* larger youth outreach programming. Further school resources, including a digital copy of this entire guide, can be found at ***http://schools.asexualoutreach.org/***
For additional help including aces in your school and classes or to bring a speaker to your school, you can contact us by email at ***schools@asexualoutreach.org*** or by phone *(toll-free)* at ***1-855-5-ASEXUAL (1-855-527-3982)***.

Glossary

INDEX

A	4
B - E	6
G	7, 8
G - K	8
L - P	9
P - Q	10
Q - R	11
S	12
S - Z	13

This glossary contains a list of definitions for terms that are relevant to the asexual spectrum, as well as descriptions for some symbols that are relevant to the ace community. Because the ace community is constantly evolving and because new terms continue to emerge, a supplementary online glossary will be continually updated at http://schools.asexualoutreach.org/glossary/

Glossary

- **Ace** — *A shorthand term used to reference the asexual spectrum or an individual who identifies on it.*

- **Acephobia** — *Prejudice or discrimination against aces and/or the asexual spectrum.*

- **Aesthetic Attraction** — *An appreciation of or attraction toward a person's surface level attributes that is not necessarily connected to sexual, romantic, or platonic desires.*

- **Allosexual** — *An individual who does not identify on the asexual spectrum. Also known as "z-sexual."*

- **Amatonormativity** — *The societal assumption that monogamous amorous relationships are the highest form of relationships and are a universally shared goal for all people. Amatonormativity values, prefers, and normalizes amorous relationships over non-amorous relationships. While this societal norm is harmful to all people, it is especially harmful to individuals on the aromantic spectrum.*

- **Androromantic** — *A person who experiences romantic attraction to male-identified people, regardless of their own gender. Used most often by genderqueer/non-binary individuals.*

- **Aporomantic** — *See "lithromantic."*

- **Aro** - *A shorthand for aromantic.*

- **Aroflux** - *A person who fluctuates between periods of experiencing romantic attraction and periods of not experiencing romantic attraction with varying intensity throughout.*

Glossary

- **Aromantic** - *A person who does not experience romantic attraction.*

- **Aromantic Spectrum** - *The collection of romantic orientations and identities that do not fit within the bounds of what is traditionally considered "romantic." The aromantic spectrum includes aromantic, demi-romantic, grayromantic, quoiromantic, as well as many other identities.*

- **Arousal** - *A physical response to stimuli.*

- **Asexual** - *A person who experiences little or no sexual attraction to anyone, and/or does not experience desire for sexual contact.*

- **Asexual Flag** - *The asexual flag consists of four equal horizontal stripes, colored black, gray, white, and purple. Black represents asexuality, gray represents gray-asexuality, demisexuality and the rest of the gray area, white represents non-ace identities, and purple represents community.*

- **Asexual Spectrum** — *The collection of sexual orientations and identities that encompasses asexuality and all of the identities in the gray area - i.e. all sexual orientations and identities that fall under the 'ace umbrella'*

- **Asexy** — *A slang term that describes someone or something that is made more attractive by their/its lack of sexuality.*

- **AVEN** — *An abbreviation for the Asexual Visibility and Education Network – a prominent online ace forum that fostered one of the first ace communities.*

Glossary

- ▼ **Biromantic** — *A person who experiences romantic attraction to two or more genders. Analogous to bisexual.*

- ▼ **Black Ring** - *A common ace symbol that - when worn on the middle finger of the right hand - indicates that a person is ace.*

- ▼ **Cake** - *Commonly referenced in relation to the asexual spectrum, often as a joke. Originated on an ace forum discussion as an answer to "What's better than sex?"*

- ▼ **Compulsory Sexuality** — *The pervasive societal belief that everyone past a certain age experiences sexual attraction and that everyone can and should want to engage in sexual activity.*

- ▼ **Corrective Rape** — *Sexual assault/rape intended to change the victim's sexual orientation.*

- ▼ **Demi** - *A shorthand term for demisexual or demiromantic.*

- ▼ **Demiromantic** — *A person who does not experience romantic attraction toward someone unless they have established a close emotional connection with that person.*

- ▼ **Demisexual** — *A person who does not experience sexual attraction toward someone unless they have established a close emotional connection with that person.*

- ▼ **Emotional Attraction** - *Describes the attraction to another person because of their emotions and, by extension, their personality.*

Glossary

- **Grace** — *A slang term for gray-asexual.*

- **Gray-A** — *A shorthand for gray-asexual or gray-aromantic*

- **Gray Area** — *The area "between" asexuality and z-sexuality on a spectrum. The gray area includes gray-asexuality, demisexuality, and other "gray" identities.*

- **Gray-Asexual** — *A person who experiences sexual attraction rarely, only under specific circumstances, without libido/sex-drive, or without enough strength to act on that attraction. This can also describe someone who fluctuates between periods of experiencing sexual attraction and periods of not experiencing sexual attraction.*

- **Gray-Aromantic** — *A term often used to describe someone who falls between aromantic and romantic. Some people also use quoiromantic and other labels to express that they do not find romantic attraction useful as concept, or that they experience romantic attraction, but that it is unclear and is difficult to identify how that attraction works.*

- **Graysexual** — *A shorthand for gray-asexual.*

- **GSD** — *Gender and Sexual Diversity. An alternative to the LGBTQ+ acronym.*

- **GSM** — *Gender and sexual minorities. An alternative to the LGBTQ+ acronym.*

- **GSRM** — *Gender, sexual, and romantic minorities. An alternative to the LGBTQ+ acronym.*

Glossary

- **Gynoromantic** — A person who experiences romantic attraction to female-identified people, regardless of their own gender. Used most often by genderqueer/non-binary individuals.

- **Heteroromantic** — A person who experiences romantic attraction to people with a different gender than their own. Analogous to heterosexual.

- **Heteronormativity** — The belief that people fall into exactly two distinct and complementary genders (male and female), and that heterosexuality is the only sexual orientation, or the only normal sexual orientation.

- **Heterosexism** — Discrimination against people who are not heterosexual, heteroromantic, and cisgender. See heteronormativity.

- **Homoromantic** — A person who experiences romantic attraction to people with the same gender as their own. Analogous to homosexual.

- **Hypoactive Sexual Desire Disorder (HSDD)** — An outdated and controversial medical disorder that is listed in the DSM-III and DSM-IV that pathologizes the asexual spectrum.

- **Kink** — A non-conventional means of pleasure that is often but not necessarily sexual. Some aces have kinks.

- **Kinsey Scale** — A popular mid-20th century model that categorized human sexuality as a spectrum from heterosexual to homosexual with degrees of bisexuality between the two. Asexual people were classified as **"Group X"** and were not included on the scale.

Glossary

- **Libido** — *A psychological desire for sexual activity and/or sexual pleasure. This desire can emerge alongside or independent of sexual attraction; therefore, many aces can experience libido.*

- **Lithromantic** — *A person who experiences romantic attraction but does not care about, need, or want reciprocation. Romantic attraction may fade once reciprocated; and some lithromantic individuals are romance repulsed. Also called "akoi(ne) romantic" and "aporomantic."*

- **MOGAI** — *Marginalized Orientations, Gender Alignments, and Intersex. An alternative to the LGBTQ+ acronym.*

- **Nonlibidoist** — *A person who does not experience libido or sex drive.*

- **Panromantic** — *A person who experiences romantic attraction to people of any gender.*

- **Pathologization** — *The act of viewing or treating something as medically or psychologically abnormal. The asexual spectrum is often pathologized.*

- **Platonic Attraction** — *The desire to deeply know someone or to befriend someone in a way that is more emotionally intimate than a typical friendship. This attraction is non-sexual and non-romantic in nature, but results in the desire to be around someone in a friendly capacity.*

- **Poly** — *A shorthand for polyamorous.*

Glossary

- **Polyamorous** — Practicing, desiring, or accepting intimate relationships that are not sexually or romantically exclusive with the knowledge and consent of everyone involved. Not to be confused with polyromantic.

- **Polyromantic** — A person who experiences romantic attraction to multiple but not to all genders. Not to be confused with polyamorous.

- **Pomosexual** — A person who rejects, denies, avoids, or does not fit into any sexual orientation label.

- **Primary Attraction** — Attraction that is experienced upon first meeting or observing someone.

- **Queer** — An originally pejorative term referring to trans individuals and to individuals with same-sex attractions/desires. This term has been reclaimed by many within the LGBTQ+ community. Some aces identify as queer while others do not.

- **Queerplatonic (QP) Relationship** — An intimate relationship that is not romantic and that is not adequately described by friendship.

- **Quirkyplatonic/Quasiplatonic Relationship** — See "Queerplatonic Relationship."

- **QUILTBAG** — Queer/Questioning, Undecided, Intersex, Lesbian, Trans, Bisexual, Asexual, Gay/Genderqueer. An alternative to the LGBTQ+ acronym.

- **Quoiromantic** — *A label (and sometimes identity) that people use to express that they do not find romantic attraction useful as concept, or to express that they experience romantic attraction, but that the attraction is unclear, or that it is difficult to identify how that attraction works.*

- **Rape Culture** — *The social expectations that encourage sexual aggression, promote the social acceptance of sexual assault, and cause individuals to deny the importance or the recognition of sexual assault.*

- **Recipromantic** — *A person that can only experience romantic attraction to those who have first expressed romantic attraction to them.*

- **Relationship Anarchy** — *The belief that no kinds of intimate relationships are inherently superior to others despite being more highly valued in society. In practice, relationship anarchy involves forming relationships that are not bound by rules aside from what those involved agree on.*

- **Romantic Attraction** — *Describes how one is drawn to others in a strictly "romantic" way. As with sexual attraction, people who experience romantic attraction often experience it toward a specific gender or toward multiple genders.*

- **Romantic Orientation** — *An individual's pattern of romantic attraction, often toward a specific gender, toward multiple genders, or to nobody at all.*

Glossary

- **Secondary Attraction** - *Attraction that develops after knowing an individual personally for some time.*

- **Sensual Attraction** - *Describes the urge to be physically intimate with someone in a non-sexual manner.*

- **Sex-Averse** — *Describes a person who is averse to sex, and who may or may not be repulsed by sex.*

- **Sex Drive** — *See "Libido."*

- **Sex-Indifferent** — *Describes a person who has neither a desire to participate in sexual activity nor a desire to avoid it.*

- **Sex Positivity** — *A movement or ideology that values all forms of sex between enthusiastically consenting adults. Sex positivity often fails to value a lack of sexual activity.*

- **Sex-Repulsed** — *Describes a person who experiences repulsion to sex. This person may only be repulsed by sexual activity that includes them, or they may be repulsed by sexual activity in general.*

- **Sexual Attraction** — *Describes how one is drawn to others "sexually", and often results in a desire for sexual contact with those others. It is commonly defined as a sexual urge that is directed at or caused by a specific person, a specific gender, or specific genders that occurs outside of a sexual situation or context.*

- **Sexual Orientation** — *An individual's pattern of sexual attraction, often toward a specific gender, toward multiple genders, or to nobody at all.*

Glossary

▼ **Squish** — *The platonic or non-romantic equivalent of a crush. A very strong desire to get to know someone, be their friend, and spend time with them.*

▼ **Zucchini** — *A slang term for a queerplatonic partner.*

▼ **Z-Romantic** — *An individual who does not identify on the aromantic spectrum.*

▼ **Z-Sexual** — *An individual who does not identify on the asexual spectrum. Also known as "allosexual."*

ℹ️ This Ace Inclusion Guide for High Schools is a part of *Asexual Outreach's* larger youth outreach programming. Further school resources, including a digital copy of this entire guide, can be found at **http://schools.asexualoutreach.org/**
For additional help including aces in your school and classes or to bring a speaker to your school, you can contact us by email at ***schools@asexualoutreach.org*** or by phone *(toll-free)* at **1-855-5-ASEXUAL (1-855-527-3982)**.

DESIGN BY: ALEKSANDER ROMERO

www.ingramcontent.com/pod-product-compliance
Lightning Source LLC
Chambersburg PA
CBHW042321150426
43192CB00001B/9